j781
L

LACEY, Marion
Picture book of musical instruments, by
Marion Lacey; illus. by Leonard Weisgard.
N. Y., Lothrop [c1942] 55p. illus. 3.94 lib.

RELATED
BOOKS IN
CATALOG
UNDER
}
1. *Musical instruments*

Twenty-four instruments are described
with full-page drawing of each.   cc 5-7

77142   My74

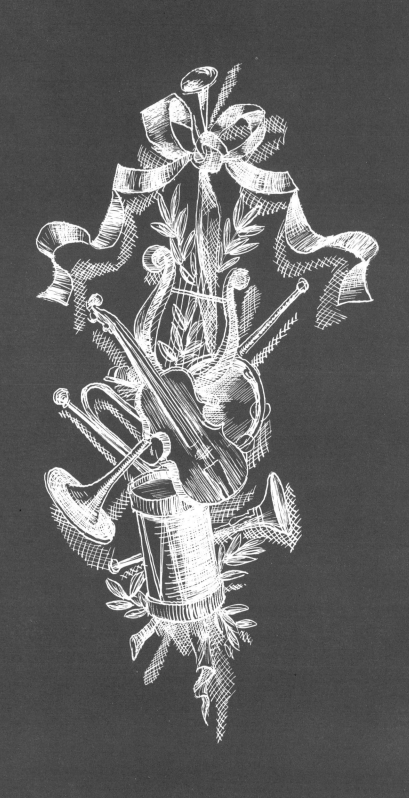

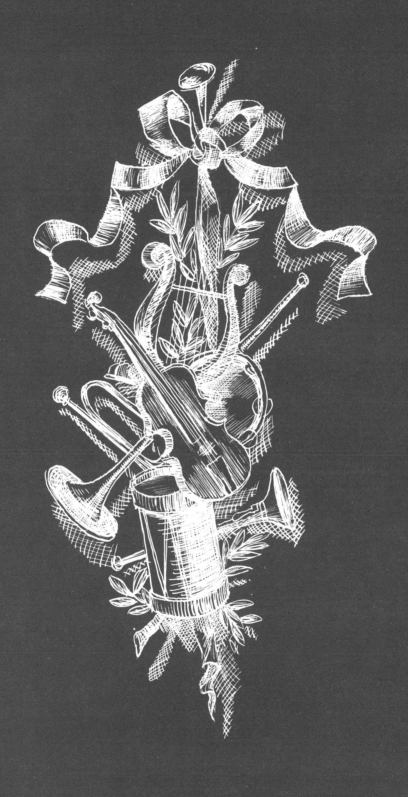

Picture Book of Musical Instruments

PICTURE
BOOK
OF
MUSICAL
INSTRUMENTS

by

MARION LACEY

Illustrated by
LEONARD WEISGARD

LOTHROP, LEE & SHEPARD CO.
BOSTON   NEW YORK

Copyright, 1942

by

LOTHROP, LEE & SHEPARD CO.

Printed in the United States of America

16 17 18 19 20 78 77 76 75 74 73

CONTENTS

FOREWORD

Music means more if you know how it is made. Known and unknown craftsmen for thousands of years have contributed their skill and artistry to the development of the modern orchestra, and the pleasure we experience in listening to music today is greatly increased by some knowledge of the instruments that make it.

This book condenses more fascinating information on the subject than any I have seen. The full page illustrations, drawn with exquisite artistry, show clearly the distinguishing details of each instrument; and the charming vignettes suggest the romantic sources from which they have evolved.

ALEXANDER RICHTER, *Chairman*

Department of Music, High School of Music and Art, New York City

THE STRINGED INSTRUMENTS

In the orchestra all the instruments played with bows are called the strings. These are the violin, viola, violoncello and double bass. All of them are descendants of the old viols the troubadours used to play as they went about from village to village and castle to castle, performing for festive events. These instruments were of various sizes and shapes, and were extremely crude. Down through the centuries changes and improvements were made, until at last the great Italian masters of the seventeenth century produced instruments which were so nearly perfect that to this day no one has been able to improve on them.

From 1560 to 1760 the little town of Cremona, in Italy, was the violin center for the whole world. Amati, Guarnerius and Stradivarius were the best of the craftsmen of that period and are the ones most remembered today. Stradivarius was the greatest of them all. Many artists today play his instruments, and more than four hundred of his violins are still in existence.

THE VIOLIN

A violin is beautiful to look at, as well as lovely to hear. It contains about seventy pieces of wood, put together with glue and then varnished. Its four strings are stretched over the bridge, fastened at one end to the tailpiece and at the other end to pegs, which are turned to tune the instrument.

The bow is as important to a violinist as breath is to a singer. A fine violinist must have a fine bow. It was more than a hundred years after the violin was perfected that François Tourte of Paris designed the bow that is still used today. With the heavier bow used before his time, it was impossible for violinists to play as brilliantly as our great artists do.

The violin bow is about 29 inches long. It has about 150 hairs, which can be loosened or tightened by turning a screw in the end of the bow. The back of the bow, or stick, must be strong but elastic. Pernambuco wood from Brazil is used in the finest bows.

THE VIOLA

Most of the important makers of violins also made violas. The viola is made in the same way as the violin, but is one-fifth larger and is tuned a fifth lower. It is the alto to the violin's soprano.

The earliest members of the string family all went under the name of viols. These were the instruments of the troubadours. They were of different sizes and shapes. Some were played with bows, some were plucked like a guitar, some were played like a hurdy-gurdy. As orchestras began to be formed many of these early instruments were dropped, and the four that we have in our string section today were finally determined to be the most satisfactory for orchestra use.

During the seventeenth and eighteenth centuries it was the fashion for royal personages to have as a part of their household a composer of music and a group of musicians to play the music he wrote. Much of this music was what is called "chamber music"—music to be played in intimate gatherings by small groups or string quartets. It was as a member of these string quartets that the viola first assumed an important part of its own.

THE VIOLONCELLO

The name of this instrument comes from the Italian word, *violone*, which means double bass, and the word ending, *'cello*, which means small. In America it is usually called by the name 'cello.

The ancestor of the violoncello was the viola da gamba, or knee fiddle, which was held gripped between the knees of the player. Today the 'cello is held between the knees, but rests on a spike on the floor.

The tone of the 'cello is full and rich. When played by a master, its tone can be as sweet and almost as light as a violin, and its deeper notes are warm and vibrant. Like the other stringed instruments, the 'cello is sometimes played by plucking the strings with the fingers. This method of playing is called pizzicato, and is particularly effective on the 'cello.

Some of the earliest of the great violinists liked to have a 'cello accompany them when they played. Early church choirs also used 'cellos to blend with the voices in the bass.

THE DOUBLE BASS

The largest of the stringed instruments is the double bass. It is so tall that its player must stand while he plays. The strings are heavy and long, and require strong fingers to press them down. Its bow is shorter and much thicker than those of the other stringed instruments.

The shoulders of the double bass are more sloping than those of the other members of the string family. It more nearly resembles the old viols the troubadours played. Most double basses have four strings, but some have only three and some have five.

The voice of the double bass is one of the lowest in the entire orchestra. Its tone is heavy and gruff, and helps to make a firm background for the melodies of the other instruments.

THE WOOD-WIND INSTRUMENTS

The wood-wind instruments include the flute and piccolo, oboe, English horn, clarinet and bassoon. The saxophone also is usually included in this group. In some form these instruments have been in existence for many centuries, and there are numerous legends about the first discovery that blowing through a reed would create a musical sound.

The best known of these is the story of the god Pan. One day, a nymph he was pursuing was changed into a reed by the Naiads. The fat and jolly Pan, tired after the chase, sat down, sighing over the reeds. To his surprise, he discovered they gave forth a musical sound, and forgetting his disappointment, he amused himself by blowing tunes upon the pipes he fashioned from the reeds.

Originally all the wood winds were made of wood. Now, however, metal is often used. All of them have reed mouthpieces except the flute and piccolo. It is the vibration of the reed which gives the wood-winds their peculiar tone, thin and nasal, penetrating and rather sad.

12

THE FLUTE

There have been periods in history when it was almost essential for anyone who claimed to be a gentleman to be able to play upon the flute. Several members of royal families have also been accomplished flutists. Henry VIII played the instrument. Frederick the Great of Prussia was an enthusiastic flutist, and composed music for it. Early flutes were blown from the end. These were called flageolets, beak flutes, or recorders. The recorder was particularly popular in England and for that reason is often called the English flute. After 1700 the side-blown or transverse flute replaced the end-blown instrument.

The flute that is used today was developed about a hundred years ago by Theobald Boehm, a German, who invented the system of keys and levers which makes it possible to play the instrument in any key. Originally it was made of wood, but now it usually is made of nickel-silver, in three pieces which fit together to form a long tube. The mouthpiece is at the side, near one end, and the instrument is played by blowing the breath across the opening.

The tone of the flute is silvery and clear, and has a liquid quality. It often represents bird notes, and when it is used as an obbligato with a soprano solo it is sometimes difficult to tell which is the voice and which the instrument.

The piccolo is the little brother of the flute. It is half as long, and plays high notes that are beyond the range of the flute. Its voice is shrill and piercing, and altogether it makes a great deal of noise for so small an instrument. For that reason it is sometimes called the "imp" of the orchestra.

THE OBOE

The oboe got its name from the French word, *hautbois,* which means "high wood." It was given this name because the instrument is made of wood and has a high pitch. Hautboy is the old English form of this French word, and is pronounced ho-boy. The oboe's voice is the highest of the double-reed mouthpiece group, which also includes the English horn and the bassoon.

All of these double-reed instruments are descended from the shawm, which was brought to Europe from the Orient by the Crusaders. The shawm was in common use in the Orient. It was the instrument the snake charmers used. Shepherd boys played it as they watched their sheep. It furnished music for dancing. Its weird, mysterious tone was heard in religious ceremonies in the temples.

The oboe is a tube of black wood about two feet long, with a bell-shaped end. Its mouthpiece is made of two thin pieces of cane which vibrate together. It is one of the most difficult instruments to play. Only a small stream of air can be blown through the opening between the two pieces of reed, and this makes it impossible for the performer to play for a very long period without stopping to breathe.

The reedy, plaintive tone of the oboe is easy to distinguish in the orchestra. There are a number of instruments many times its size, but because of the penetrating quality of the tone, two oboes can hold their own against an entire orchestra.

THE ENGLISH HORN

No one seems to know just where the English horn got its name, for it is not English and it is not a horn. One story is that its name was suggested by the resemblance of its tone to that of the old English hornpipe, which shepherds used to play.

The English horn has the same ancestors as the oboe, and, like the oboe, it is made of wood. But there are also marked differences between them. The English horn is half again as large as the oboe, and is pitched a fifth lower. Its double-reed mouthpiece is fastened to a curved tube, and the open end of the instrument is rounded instead of flaring. Neither the English horn nor the oboe can be made satisfactorily of metal, because metal does not give the proper tone. Grenadilla wood from South Africa is the best material. It is very hard, and does not warp or crack easily.

The tone of the English horn is dreamy and rather melancholy. It has a far-away quality, and is less piercing than that of the oboe.

THE CLARINET

The ancient Greeks created the instrument which was the forefather of the clarinet, but it was not until about 1690, when an instrument maker named Johann Christoph Denner invented improvements which gave it a better tone and made it easier to play, that it became a member in good standing of the orchestra. Theobald Boehm made further improvements to develop the instrument we have today.

The clarinet is a tube made of metal, ebonite or wood, with the open end shaped like a bell. Its mouthpiece has a single reed, instead of the double reed of the other wood winds, which is held in place by metal bands and screws. It has the greatest range of any of the wood-wind instruments, and its tone varies in different parts of its compass. The lower notes are mellow; the middle tones, clear and expressive; the upper notes, brilliant and sometimes almost shrill.

Most large orchestras also include a bass clarinet. This is twice as long as the soprano instrument, and its bell curves up and out. It has a grave and solemn tone.

THE BASSOON

The bassoon is sometimes called the clown of the orchestra, because many composers have written for it gay little tunes and dances which sound ridiculous coming from the large, clumsy-looking instrument. The Italian name for the bassoon is *fagotto,* which means bundle of sticks. It was given this name because it looks rather like two big sticks tied together. The tube of the instrument is so long—nearly eight feet—that in order to make it easier to handle, it was necessary to double it back upon itself. The double bassoon, which plays an octave lower and has a tube nearly sixteen feet long, is doubled back twice, so that it looks like four sticks in a bundle.

Bassoons usually are made of curly maple or rosewood, with nickel-silver or silver-plated keys, and have a curved brass tube which holds the double-reed mouthpiece.

Most large orchestras use two bassoons and one double bassoon.

THE SAXOPHONE

Although we usually think of the saxophone as a modern instrument and identify it chiefly with jazz bands, it was invented by Adolph Sax more than a century ago and was used in symphony orchestras before jazz was ever heard of. Not as much serious music has been written for it as for some of the other wind instruments, but modern composers are using it more and more in their orchestrations.

The saxophone is neither wholly a wood-wind nor wholly a brass-wind instrument, but a mixture of the two. It is made of brass, but has a single-reed mouthpiece similar to that of the clarinet. It is shaped rather like a big Dutch pipe. Probably part of its great popularity is due to the fact that a beginner can learn to play the saxophone fairly quickly.

The tone of the saxophone is a blend between the wood-winds and the brasses. It is brighter than that of the wood-winds, but not so brilliant as that of the brasses. Its tone has a beauty all its own.

THE BRASS-WIND INSTRUMENTS

The brass section of the orchestra is made up of the trumpets, French horns, trombones and tubas. These instruments have a thrilling background. Centuries before the modern symphony orchestra was dreamed of, their ancestors were heard on battlefields, in royal courts, in the hunt, in religious ceremonies, and an echo of all this seems to sound for us in their music when we hear these instruments today.

The instruments in this group, like those of the strings, went through a long period of change. In the beginning most of them were made of horn, and could produce only a few notes. In the United States, at the time of the Civil War, some of these brasses were made with the bell pointing backward over the shoulder. This was done so that the music of the band, at the head of the column, would carry better to the marching men behind. The modern instruments have the bells pointing forward.

THE TRUMPET

The trumpet is an instrument with a long and proud history. Thousands of years ago it was used in religious ceremonies and on the battlefields. The ancient Chinese and Indians used it to frighten away evil spirits. The Romans used it for military signals; and the Bible story tells us that the walls of Jericho fell when Joshua's trumpeters blew a blast. For hundreds of years trumpets could be used only in the service of royalty. The rank of the royal personages was shown by the number of trumpeters who went before them, clearing the way with their fanfares. These early trumpets were not like the ones we have today, but were long, straight instruments, such as we see in old pictures of royal courts.

The modern trumpet has about four feet of brass tubing, coiled into oblong shape and ending in a bell. Its mouthpiece is cup-shaped. There are over two hundred separate parts in the instrument. It has three valves, operated by the right hand, which make it possible to play all the notes in the scale. The tone of the trumpet is brilliant and martial; its voice is that of one accustomed to giving commands.

THE FRENCH HORN

The French horn came to us from the hunting fields of France, where it was used to give signals in the chase. Some of these signals were really little musical airs. Later these airs were used by composers in writing for the orchestra, and the French horn first entered the orchestra to play these parts. Its earliest ancestor was the Hebrew shofar, made of a ram's horn, which has been used for more than six thousand years in certain Jewish ceremonies.

There are more than twelve feet of tubing in the French horn, coiled into a circular shape and ending in a large bell. Its mouthpiece is shaped like a funnel. A system of valves, operated by the left hand, makes it possible to play a chromatic scale on the instrument.

The French horn is a very important member of the brass family of the orchestra. It can have mellow, velvety tones that blend well with the strings and woodwinds; or it can have a powerful, brilliant tone that combines with the other brasses. It is considered the most difficult of all the brass instruments to play.

THE TROMBONE

Trombone, in Italian, means "big trumpet," and for hundreds of years the instrument was considered just that. When it was introduced into England it was given the name "sackbut." This word came from the Spanish and means "a pump," so it is easy to understand why the name was given to the instrument we call the slide trombone. With the invention of the slide principle, however, the trombone came to be recognized as an entirely separate instrument.

A trombone has no keys or valves; the player changes the pitch by pulling the slide in and out with his right hand. Bass trombones have a valve which makes it possible for them to play lower notes in the scale than the regular tenor instrument.

Some composers have believed the trombone to be the finest of all the wind instruments, and even too noble to be used except in music of great power. It can express a chant or lament equally as well as a majestic or martial theme. Outside the symphony, it is one of the most popular instruments in dance bands.

THE TUBA

The tuba is a descendant of a curious instrument called the serpent, which was popular in Europe in the seventeenth century. In some of Shakespeare's plays musicians appear playing this instrument, which was given its name because its curved tube looked like a snake. The bass voice of the orchestra for many years was supplied by the serpent and various other instruments related to it. Finally, in the middle of the nineteenth century, Adolphe Sax (who also invented the saxophone) developed the tuba, which took the place of these other instruments as the bass of the brass section.

The tuba is made of coiled brass tubing, ending in a huge bell. Its large mouthpiece is shaped like a cup. With its four valves any note in the scale can be played. The tone of the tuba is deep and gruff, and has been compared to the rumble of distant thunder. It forms a solid bass to the harmony of the trombones.

THE PERCUSSION INSTRUMENTS

The percussion section of the orchestra includes all the instruments that are played by striking with a mallet or stick, and also the cymbals, which are played by striking one against the other. Some of the instruments have no definite tone pitch, and are used only for marking rhythm. Others do have a definite pitch or scale, and are used for harmony as well as rhythm.

Rhythm is as important a part of music as melody. In primitive music it is more important, and drums are the chief instruments used in such music. There has never been a time when drums were unknown. African tribes beat drums in ceremonies of war and worship. To this day messages are sent long distances through the jungles by the varying rhythms of the drum beat. From the jungle to the concert stage is a long journey, but drums are also important members of the symphony orchestra.

There are many kinds of percussion instruments. Some large orchestras have as many as eight players in this section. This part of the orchestra is often called "the battery."

THE TYMPANI

When the Crusaders returned to Europe from the Orient in the thirteenth century, they brought with them, slung over the necks of their horses, pairs of drums which looked like the halves of a great ball. These were the ancestors of the tympani, or kettledrums, which are the most important percussion instruments of the orchestra. They are made of brass, with sheepskin heads which are tightened or loosened to raise or lower the tone.

The tympani are the only drums which have a definite pitch and are used as part of the harmony as well as to mark rhythm. Different qualities of tone are obtained by using mallets with hard or soft heads. A tympanist must have a perfect sense of rhythm and a good ear for tuning.

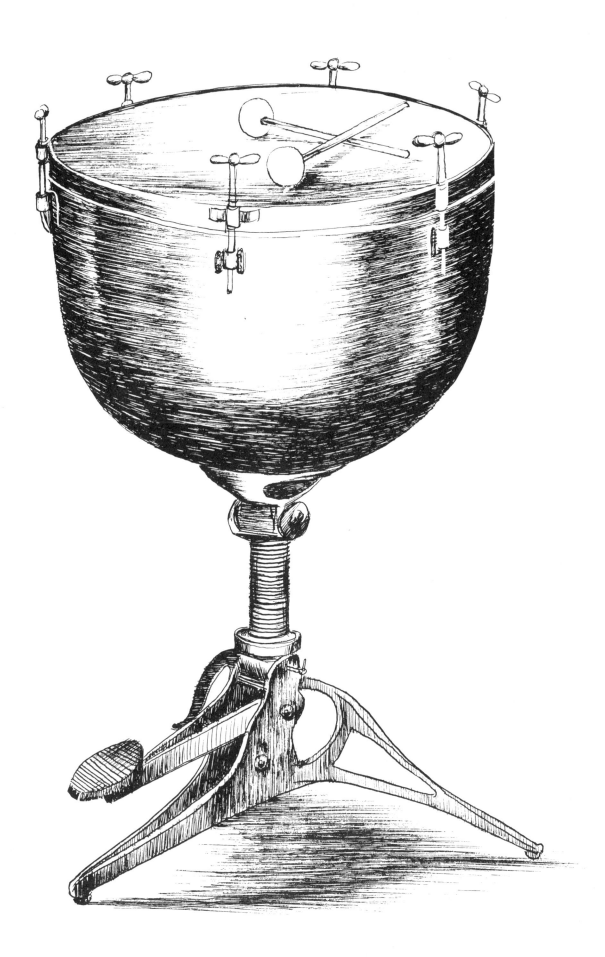

THE SNARE DRUM

In the Revolutionary and Civil Wars the drummer boy was a necessary member of the military organization, and the roll of his drum was used for giving signals. The crisp, martial tone of his drum, like that of the modern snare drum, came from the catgut strings, called "snares," stretched across one of the heads, which gave the drum its name. When the snares are loosened the tone is muffled and gives a mournful effect.

THE BASS DRUM

The big bass drum is a familiar sight whenever a band marches by on parade, and its boom-boom-boom-boom makes everyone step in time with the music. The bass drum does not have a definite pitch, and in the orchestra it is used for marking rhythm and for certain effects of tone.

THE CYMBALS

The best cymbals are made in Turkey. They are two hollowed-out discs, hammered by hand from bronze. It takes great skill to make the cymbals touch each other at just the right place and with the proper degree of force. It is exciting to watch the player get ready for his cue. His playing requires great exactness of timing —if the crash of the cymbals should come in at the wrong moment, the mistake cannot be hidden.

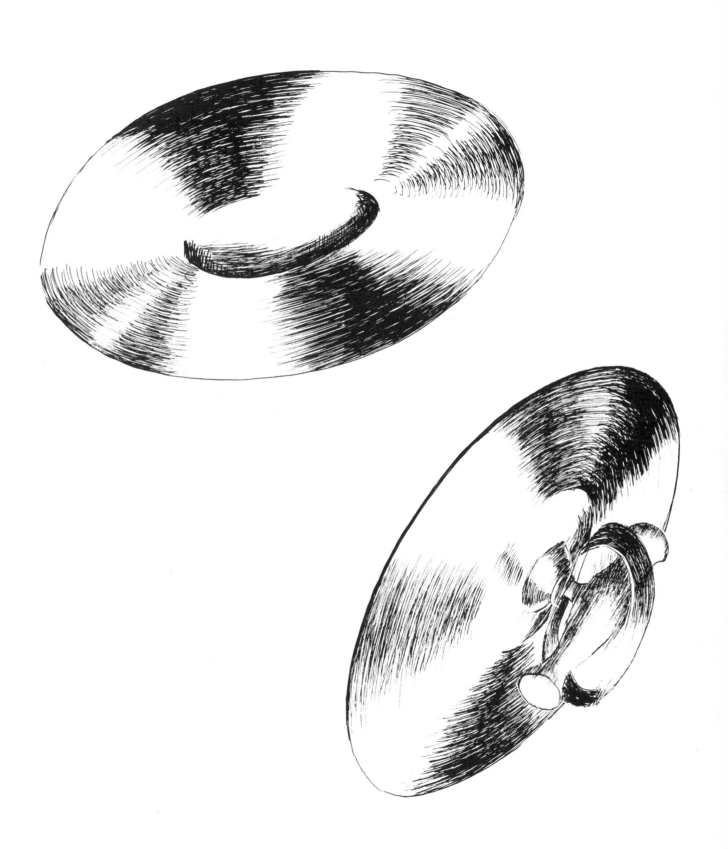

THE CHIMES

The giant bells in the carillons in church towers would hardly be practical for use in an orchestra, since they weigh up to twenty thousand pounds. But composers wanted to produce the effect of those bells in their music. They found that metal tubes from one to two and one-half inches in diameter and from four to six feet long would reproduce the quality of tone and pitch of all but the lowest notes of the big carillons. These chimes, made of eighteen such tubes and struck with a wooden mallet, are used in orchestras for the bell effects.

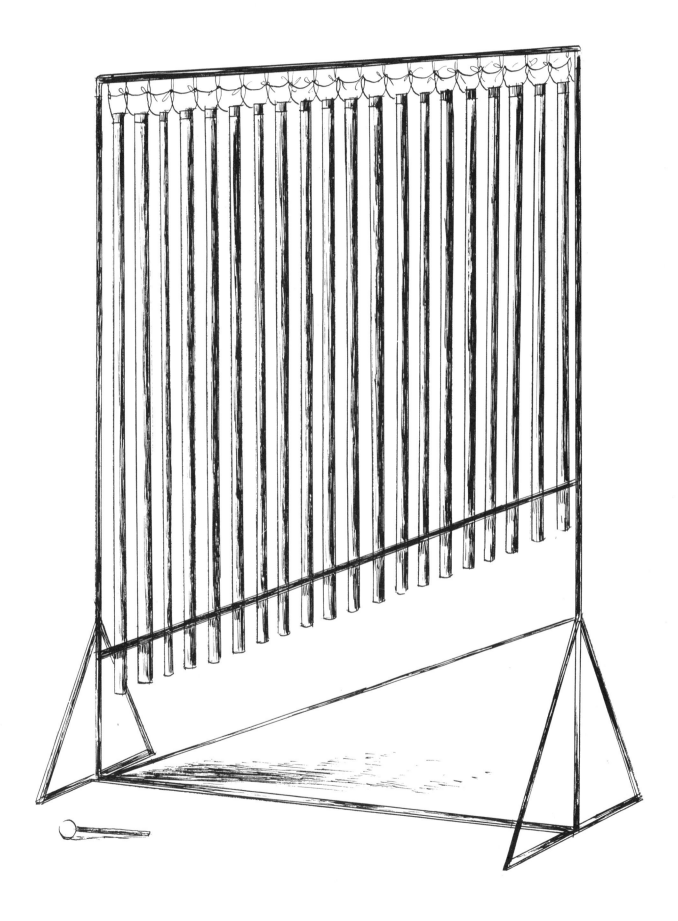

THE XYLOPHONE

The xylophone is made of a series of wooden bars, arranged in two rows, which are graduated in size to produce the notes of the scale. It has a range of about four octaves. The wood is very hard, and when the bars are struck with hard mallets they give a brief, brilliant sound.

The rosewood which is used for the bars of the xylophone comes from Central or South America. It ranges in color from reddish-brown to black.

THE TAMBOURINE

The tambourine is a very ancient instrument. It was known long ago all over southern Europe, but we usually think of it as being Spanish, because it is so popular in Spanish music. It is really a small drum with only one head. Metal discs are fastened loosely on the rim and give a jingling sound when the instrument is shaken or struck with the hand.

THE CASTANETS

Castanets are also Spanish. They are small wooden or ebonite clappers, held in the hands, and are used to mark rhythm. Their crisp clicking is a familiar sound in Spanish dances, and it is often said that few people who are not Spanish born can ever learn to use them properly.

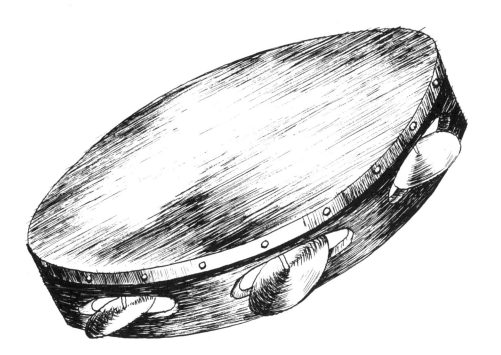

THE HARP

The harp we know today is very different from the instrument the boy David played for King Saul. But a form of harp was known even long before that time. There are many stories about its beginnings. One of them is that some unknown hunter noticed that when he had shot his arrow, the string of the bow continued to vibrate with a musical sound. Perhaps he amused himself on winter evenings by adding more strings, which gave him other notes, and he found that the chords he could play made a pleasant accompaniment to his songs. No one knows who had the idea for the first harp; but through the centuries many men added to it and improved it until they developed the beautiful instrument we see on the concert platform today.

The harp does not always appear with the orchestra. A great many musical scores do not call for it at all. Neither is it a member of what is called the string section of the orchestra, for it is not played with a bow, but the strings are plucked with the thumb and first three fingers. There are forty-seven strings, and seven foot pedals which change the pitch so that music in any key can be played.

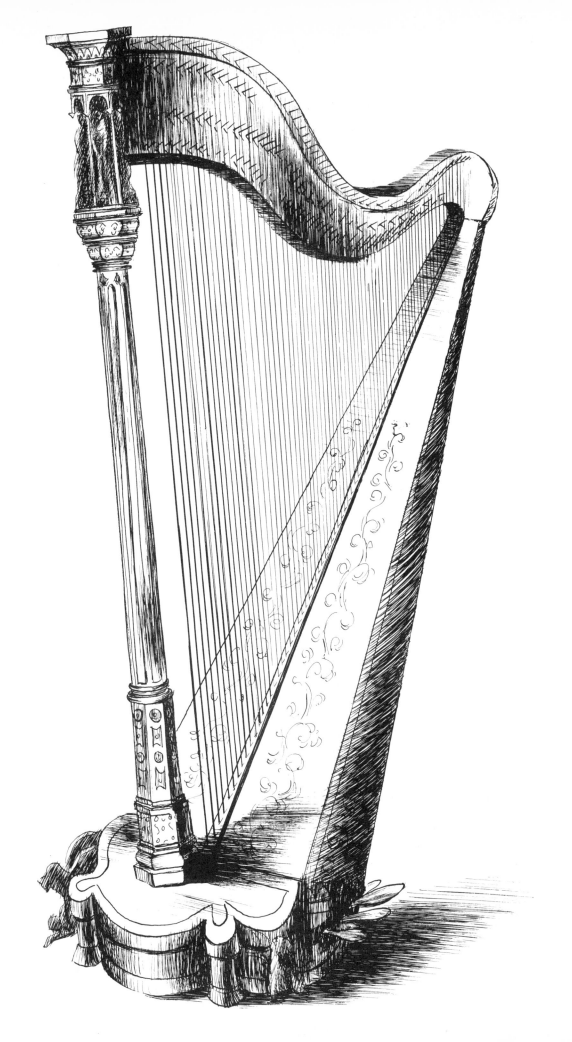

THE PIANO

Bartolomeo Cristofori, a harpsichord maker in Florence, Italy, invented the piano in 1709. He called the new instrument "pianoforte," which means soft-loud, to indicate that it could produce both a delicate and a strong tone.

In the two centuries since that first pianoforte was made there have been countless improvements. The modern concert grand piano is an instrument that Cristofori could only have dreamed of. Its eighty-eight notes match the playing range of all the instruments in the orchestra, and it has a wider variety of tone and effects than any other instrument.

The piano is not usually a member of the symphony orchestra, but often appears with it as the solo instrument in concerti written for piano and orchestra. It is sometimes used in small orchestras, however, to provide a background and fill in for missing instruments.

| The Violin | The Viola | The Violoncello |

| The Double Bass | The Flute | The Clarinet |

| The English Horn | The Oboe | The Bassoon |

The Saxophone

The Trumpet

The French Horn

The Trombone

The Tuba

The Tympani

The Chimes

The Xylophone

The Harp

INDEX

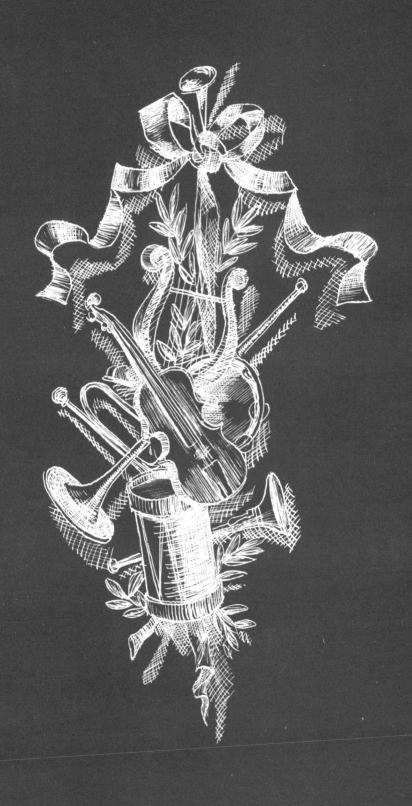

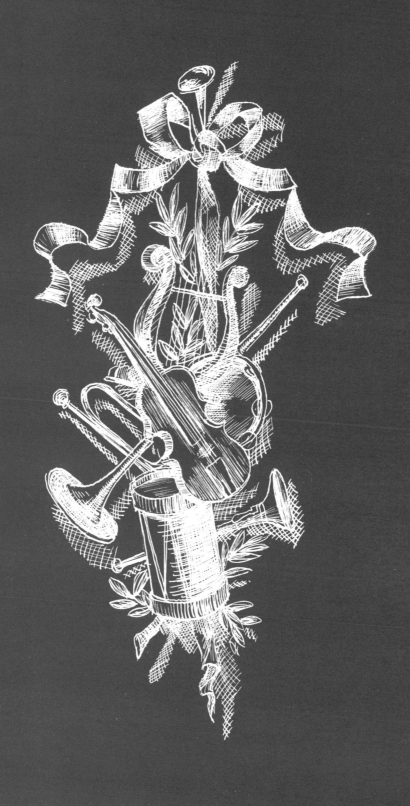